HYPE BRANDS

KITH

KENNY ABDO

Fly!
An Imprint of Abdo Zoom
abdobooks.com

abdobooks.com

Published by Abdo Zoom, a division of ABDO, P.O. Box 398166, Minneapolis, Minnesota 55439. Copyright © 2023 by Abdo Consulting Group, Inc. International copyrights reserved in all countries. No part of this book may be reproduced in any form without written permission from the publisher. Fly!™ is a trademark and logo of Abdo Zoom.

Printed in the United States of America, North Mankato, Minnesota.
052022
092022

THIS BOOK CONTAINS RECYCLED MATERIALS

Photo Credits: Alamy, Getty Images, Shutterstock, ©Ian Kennedy p.14/ CC BY-SA 2.0, ©jpellgen p.16/ CC BY-NC-ND 2.0

Production Contributors: Kenny Abdo, Jennie Forsberg, Grace Hansen
Design Contributors: Candice Keimig, Neil Klinepier, Laura Graphenteen

Library of Congress Control Number: 2021950292

Publisher's Cataloging-in-Publication Data

Names: Abdo, Kenny, author.
Title: Kith / by Kenny Abdo.
Description: Minneapolis, Minnesota : Abdo Zoom, 2023 | Series: Hype brands | Includes online resources and index.
Identifiers: ISBN 9781098228538 (lib. bdg.) | ISBN 9781644947968 (pbk.) | ISBN 9781098229375 (ebook) | ISBN 9781098229795 (Read-to-Me ebook)
Subjects: LCSH: Clothing and dress--Juvenile literature. | Brand name products--Juvenile literature. | Fashion--Social aspects--Juvenile literature. | Popular culture--Juvenile literature.
Classification: DDC 338.7--dc23

TABLE OF CONTENTS

Kith 4

Hype 8

All The Rage 14

Glossary 22

Online Resources 23

Index 24

KITH

Not many brands can put fashion, cars, and cereal together. But Kith stitches them together seamlessly.

Going strong since 2011, the brand brings together hype, pop, and **collaborations** in its own way!

Ronnie Fieg began working for his cousin David Zaken at age 13. Zaken owned the hyper-**exclusive** New York City shoe store David Z.

Fieg became the head buyer for the store in 2007. He was surrounded by popular brands like Nike, Adidas, and Chuck Taylor. It was there Fieg developed a taste for **streetwear**.

In 2010, Fieg went into business for himself. The next year, the first two Kith stores opened in Manhattan and Brooklyn.

ALL THE RAGE

At first, Kith only **stocked** sneaker brands like Adidas, Nike, and Timberland. It also included Fieg's **collaborations**.

Kith soon had its own special releases. People slept in front of the store for new limited **drops**. Kith Classics was launched in 2014. It was the brand's basic clothing line.

As a big cereal fan himself, Fieg started including cereal and ice cream bars in his Kith stores. He also wanted a place teens could both shop and hang out.

In 2016, Feig **debuted** Kithland at New York Fashion week. It was a fashion experience that showed Kith's new fashion line and exciting **collaborations**.

In 2020, Kith **collaborated** with the car company BMW. They designed a special version of the M4 Competition model. Only 150 were made, making it hyper-**exclusive**.

Kith and Nike teamed up with the New York Knicks in 2021. A custom designed uniform was worn by the team for every Friday game. Kith brought more hype to an already exciting sport!

Kith is the top of the line for **collaborations**. Fieg himself brought together **streetwear** and sneakers, making another perfect blend to hype.

GLOSSARY

collaborate – to work with another person or group in order to do something or reach a goal.

debut – a first appearance.

drop – when something that is highly anticipated is released to the public.

exclusive – the limited release of merchandise, often with a small number available.

stock – the supply of products available for sale in a store.

streetwear – fashionable, yet casual clothing worn by followers of popular culture. It is heavily influenced by hip-hop and surf culture.

ONLINE RESOURCES

To learn more about Kith, please visit **abdobooklinks.com** or scan this QR code. These links are routinely monitored and updated to provide the most current information available.

INDEX

Adidas (brand) 11, 14

BMW 18

Chuck Taylor (brand) 11

David Z (store) 9

Fieg, Ronnie 9, 11, 13, 16, 21

Kithland 17

Knicks (team) 20

New York Fashion Week 17

Nike (brand) 11, 14, 20

stores 13, 15, 16

Timberland (brand) 14

Zaken, David 9